16. A Primer of Greek Literature. By Eugene Lawrence....................................$0 25
17. A Primer of Latin Literature. By Eugene Lawrence.. 25
18. Dieudonnée. By Geraldine Butt............. 20
19. The Time of Roses. By Geraldine Butt...... 20
20. The Jilt. By Charles Reade. Illustrated.... 20
21. The Mill of St. Herbot. By Katharine S. Macquoid.. 20
22. The House on the Beach. By George Meredith 20
23. Kate Cronin's Dowry. By Mrs. Cashel Hoey. 15
24. Peter the Great. By John Lothrop Motley... 25
25. Percy and the Prophet. By Wilkie Collins... 20
26. Cooking Receipts. From *Harper's Bazar*.... 25
27. Virginia. A Roman Sketch.................. 25
28. The Jews and their Persecutors. By Eugene Lawrence.................................... 20
29. The Sad Fortunes of the Rev. Amos Barton. By George Eliot.............................. 20
30. Mr. Gilfil's Love Story. By George Eliot..... 20
31. Janet's Repentance. By George Eliot....... 20
32. The A B C of Finance. By Simon Newcomb.. 25
33. A Primer of Mediæval Literature. By Eugene Lawrence.................................... 25
34. Warren Hastings. By Lord Macaulay........ 25
35. The Life and Writings of Addison. By Lord Macaulay.................................... 25
36. Lord Clive. By Lord Macaulay.............. 25
37. Frederic the Great. By Lord Macaulay...... 25
38. The Earl of Chatham. By Lord Macaulay.... 25
39. William Pitt. By Lord Macaulay............ 25
40. Samuel Johnson, LL.D. By Lord Macaulay.. 25
41. John Hampden.—Lord Burleigh. By Lord Macaulay.................................... 25
42. Sir William Temple. By Lord Macaulay...... 25

43. Machiavelli.—Horace Walpole. By Lord Macaulay..$0 25
44. John Milton.—Lord Byron. By Lord Macaulay 25
45. My Lady's Money. Related by Wilkie Collins 25
46. Poor Zeph! By F. W. Robinson............ 20
47. Shepherds All and Maidens Fair. By Walter Besant and James Rice........................ 25
48. Back to Back. A Story of To-Day. By Edward Everett Hale............................ 25
49. The Spanish Armada for the Invasion of England. 1587-1588. By Alfred H. Guernsey...... 20
50. Da Capo. By Anne Isabella Thackeray...... 20
51. The Bride of Landeck. By G. P. R. James... 20
52. Brother Jacob.—The Lifted Veil. By Geo. Eliot 20
53. A Shadow on the Threshold. By Mary Cecil Hay.. 20
54. David's Little Lad. By L. T. Meade.......... 25
55. Count Moltke's Letters from Russia. Translated by Grace Bigelow........................ 25
56. Constantinople. By James Bryce............ 15
57. English Literature: Romance Period. By Eugene Lawrence............................ 25
58. English Literature: Classical Period. By Eugene Lawrence.............................. 25
59. English Literature: Modern Period. By Eugene Lawrence. (*In Preparation.*)
60. Tender Recollections of Irene Macgillicuddy. 15
61. Georgie's Wooer. By Mrs. Leith-Adams..... 20
62. Seven Years and Mair. By Anna T. Sadlier.. 20
63. A Sussex Idyl. By Clementina Black........ 25
64. Goldsmith.—Bunyan.—Madame D'Arblay. By Lord Macaulay................................ 25
65. The Youth's Health-Book.................. 25
66. Reaping the Whirlwind. By Mary Cecil Hay.. 20
67. A Year of American Travel. By Jessie Benton Frémont................................. 25

68. A Primer of German Literature. By Helen S. Conant....................................$0 25
69. The Coming Man. By Charles Reade........ 20
70. Hints to Women on the Care of Property. By Alfred Walker.............................. 20
71. The Curate of Orsières. By Otto Roquette. Adapted from the German by Mary A. Robinson 20
72. The Canoe and the Flying Proa. By W. L. Alden...................................... 25
73. Back to the Old Home. By Mary Cecil Hay.. 20
74. The Lady of Launay. By Anthony Trollope. 20
75. Sir Roger de Coverley. From "The Spectator." With Notes by W. Henry Wills.......... 25
76. A Hand-Book to the Practice of Pottery Painting. By John C. L. Sparkes............. 20
77. Squire Paul. By Hans Warring. Translated by Mary A. Robinson......................... 25
78. Professor Pressensee, Materialist and Inventor. By John Esten Cooke.................... 25
79. The Romance of a Back Street. By F. W. Robinson................................... 15

☞ *"Harper's Half-Hour Series" may be obtained in flexible cloth binding, at 15 cents per volume in addition to the prices of the respective volumes in paper covers.*

Published by HARPER & BROTHERS, New York.

THE

ABC OF FINANCE;

OR,

THE MONEY AND LABOR QUESTIONS FAMILIARLY EXPLAINED TO COMMON PEOPLE, IN SHORT AND EASY LESSONS.

BY SIMON NEWCOMB, LL.D.,

U. S. NAVAL OBSERVATORY, WASHINGTON, D. C.; AUTHOR OF "POPULAR ASTRONOMY."

NEW YORK:
HARPER & BROTHERS, PUBLISHERS,
FRANKLIN SQUARE.

PREFACE.

A PART of these "lessons" appeared some time since in *Harper's Weekly*. The unexpected favor with which they were received, by being reprinted, in whole or in part, by newspapers in various sections of the country, has suggested their reproduction in a more permanent form. They are now completed, by the addition of several chapters bearing on the labor questions of the present day.

CONTENTS.

THE

ABC OF FINANCE;

OR,

THE MONEY AND LABOR QUESTIONS FAMILIARLY EXPLAINED TO COMMON PEOPLE, IN SHORT AND EASY LESSONS.

No doubt the reader thinks he knows nothing about the money and labor questions, and that they are quite beyond his understanding. If he has ever tried to learn anything, he has been so bewildered by opposing theories and opposing assertions as to feel that he knew less than he did before. He is, therefore, quite ready to leave these questions to the politicians, and to vote on them as they think best.

This ought not to be. Of course there are many profound financial principles which cannot be fully seen through without careful study, but in the issues now before the people only the A B C of the subject is involved. To understand them one only needs arithmetic enough to keep an account of the money he receives and spends, and common-sense enough not to buy a lottery ticket because just the very pair of trotting horses he wants are to be drawn in the lottery. The difficulty has been that writers and speakers dive so deeply into the principles of constitutional law and the functions of government that plain people cannot clearly follow them; and thus the said people are in the best state of mind to become the dupes of wild theorists and scheming politicians. It is the duty of every man to study subjects in which his own interests and those of the community are so deeply involved with all possible calmness, and without prejudice, that he may be able to give some good reason for the faith that is in him. The writer proposes, in this little book, not to write a treatise on the subject, but only to suggest some thoughts which may be partly new to the reader, and which, if he turns them carefully over in his mind, will enable him to form an intelligent judgment upon the issues now presented to him.

LESSON I.

WHAT SOCIETY DOES FOR THE LABORER.

I SHALL suppose myself speaking to some one who sympathizes with "labor movements" of the day, trades-unions, strikes, and so on, who thinks that capital is in some way at enmity with labor, and who believes in general that the laborer does not get his right share of the good things which he helps to produce. To one who thinks thus I wish to suggest a few new thoughts.

Whence came the shoes on your feet? The leather of which they are made came all the way from the plains of Texas; the hides were tanned with bark cut down by hardy wood-choppers hundreds, and perhaps thousands, of miles from where you live. The thread with which they are sewed has required the combined labor of farmers in Ireland or planters in the South to raise the flax and cotton, and of wood-choppers in North Carolina to raise the material for the wax with which the thread is strengthened. Drovers in Texas, tanners in Tennessee, wood-choppers in the West, manufacturers without number, with more ingenious machinery than either you or I can pretend to describe, are all busy in getting up material for the shoes which you and your children are to wear two years hence, while railroad men are planning railroads, freight-cars, and engines for bringing the materials within reach of you and your shoemaker.

If so much is true of so small an article as the shoe on your foot, how is it with every other article which surrounds you? Think of your various articles of clothing. However poor and insignificant you may be, you and your family are sheltered b some kind of a roof; and if you will climb up and examine all the materials of which that roof is made, and then learn where these materials came from, you will find that the labor of scores, nay, perhaps hundreds, of people—from the miners of Cornwall and the ship-builders of Maine to the house-carpenters who are your neighbors—has been called on to shelter you from the weather. If you are sick, you are supplied with medicine in the manufacture of which the skill of the great chemists of the world has been applied; and you never saw an industrious man so poor but that in a severe case he could avail himself of the services of a doctor in whose education the experience of whole generations of physicians had been drawn upon. The very men who complain most loudly of the oppression of labor are now in most respects better taken care of when sick than kings were a thousand years ago.

You see that the poorest laborer in the land has his wants ministered to by thousands of his fellow-men, scattered throughout the wide world, and separated by oceans the crossing of which is a marvel of human skill. How is such a result possible? It is by a system of social machinery, if I may use the expression, more wonderful and effective than any that the wildest communists ever dreamed of. In their ideal system, every man works for his neighbors of the community; but in the actual system, we may almost say that the whole world is working for every one else. Do you think there is going to be any great improvement made in the system which produces such results? No sudden one, certainly. I am so much afraid of its being injured by tinkering that I am willing to suffer anything rather than see men try to pull it to pieces in order to make it go better.

Every man who expects to make an honest living has an interest in keeping this social machinery in good working order. But there is something else in which he has a still higher interest, because without it the machine itself would cease to go, and the laborer would become a slave. That something is law and order and the right of property. Complaining people sometimes say that the laborer is no better off than he was centuries ago. So unblushing a misstatement is hardly worthy of refutation; but we may take a look back, not to refute it, but to see what the laborer of the present day owes to civilization. Could I only paint you a picture of the laborer in the time of William the Conqueror, the clothes he wore, the food he ate, the air he breathed, the hut he lived in, I think you would accept all the evils of the nineteenth century without one word of complaint. But the point I now make is, that the laborer was not then his own master, but his services, and those of his children, belonged to a lord whose battles he had to fight in war, and whose grounds he had to till in peace. Why is it not so now? Because advancing civilization, with philosophers as its mouth-pieces, proclaimed the rights of each man to be the master of his own destiny, and the owner of all property which he could gain by fair bargains with his fellow-men, while law and good government stepped in to enforce the principles of philosophy. From the right of free labor and free bargaining, thus enforced by law, arose the wonderful social machine which now places in every man's hands his share of the work of the world.

I now want you to think of just a single application of the great principle just enunciated. The same law which gives the workmen of a railroad the right to leave it when they are dissatisfied with their wages gives the owners of the railroad the right to employ whom they please to run it; and if you abolish this law, you will soon find that it will be the laborers, and not the railroad owners, who will suffer. They will belong to the railroad before the road will belong to them. No matter how much they may make others suffer, they will suffer more themselves. Thus, when men forcibly interfere with the running of the trains because they are not satisfied with the men whom the companies employ to run them, they violate the fundamental law to which they owe their freedom and the advantages which they enjoy, and take the most vigorous steps they are able to throw themselves into the condition of the laborer of past ages.

LESSON II.

CAPITAL AND LABOR.

WE frequently hear of the oppression of labor by capital, and of antagonism between these two agencies. In order to judge how much foundation there is for this notion, let us inquire what capital really is. It seems as if a large portion of the labor party look upon it as some kind of instrumentality wielded by the rich for the purpose of injuring or oppressing the poor. Really, however, capital consists simply of the accumulated wealth of the past—houses, machinery, railroads, engines, mills, and everything which in any way produces the things that we want. It is one of the most important parts of the social machine described in my last lesson. I might say, indeed, that it is the whole material part of that machine. The ships which bring flannel shirts across the ocean for you to wear in winter; the factories in which those shirts were made; the railways which transport them to your city; the warehouses in which they are stored until you are ready to buy them; the roof which covers your head, and all the machinery designed for the transportation and preservation of the food you eat, are capital. To complain of these when one is suffering for the comforts of life is as if a naked and hungry man should complain that food and clothing were his enemies. Diminish or injure this capital, and the power of everybody, the laborer included, to get clothes to wear, food to eat, and shelter from the weather, will be diminished.

Let us now go a step further. Food, clothing, and shelter are the three great wants for which we all labor. To supply these wants in the best manner, both the labor and capital of others are necessary. For instance, taking all the people of the country together, they need, we may suppose, some three millions of houses to live in. These houses must be kept in repair; and, as population increases, a hundred thousand new ones must be built every year to accommodate our increasing numbers. The more labor which is put into buildings and repairs, the more perfectly will everybody, laborers included, be sheltered. So, if the house-carpenters all strike, or in any way prevent house building and repairing from going on, there will be fewer and poorer houses to shelter the population, and some one must go with less perfect shelter than he would otherwise enjoy. Perhaps you will think that in this case the loss would fall principally upon the rich, and that it would be the rich who would have to live in smaller or worse houses, rather than the poor. But the fact is directly the contrary. The rich man is able to have just such a house as he wants, and will have it without regard to the wages of carpenters; so that whatever suffering may result from the houses not being built, or enlarged, or repaired, has to be undergone by the laboring and the poorer classes, and not by the rich.

The same thing holds true of every article of food and shelter of which the laboring classes are so much in need. Let us take some examples. In the recent riot in

Pittsburgh, an immense quantity of coal oil was destroyed by the rioters. The means of lighting the houses of our country were diminished by the quantity of oil thus destroyed. There is less oil in the market, and, in consequence of the destruction, a somewhat higher price must be paid for every gallon that is left. On whom do you think the loss will fall? On the rich? Not at all. They do not burn coal oil, and if they did, they would have their houses well lighted, no matter if they do have to pay a few cents a gallon more. It is the people with whom one cent a gallon is an important item who must economize in using the oil, and strain their eyes for want of good light; so that they are the real class who must suffer by the burning of the oil.

During the reign of the Paris Commune the Communists burned three or four houses belonging to M. Thiers, a man of great wealth. Did they damage his shelter? Not in the least. No matter how many houses he owned, he could only live in one. The people whose shelter was diminished by this destruction were not M. Thiers or his family, but the tenants who had to rent houses from him. If there were ten houses less in Paris, it was inevitable that the people must have lived in fewer houses than before.

In the Pittsburgh riot of which I have spoken, several hundred thousand bushels of wheat were burned. Somebody's supply of bread must be diminished by that movement. Whose will it be? That of the rich? Not in the slightest. They will have their full supply, no matter what it costs. Those who will suffer will be the poor, who will have to give higher prices in consequence of the destruction of the wheat. If the farm laborers should strike for higher wages, and thus diminish the supply and raise the price of grain, the result would be the same. It would be their fellow-laborers of the whole country who would have to pay the cost.

I hope you will now be able to see that all accumulated capital is for the advantage of the laborer or the non-capitalist, as well as the rich. If the capitalist expends his money in building a factory, that factory is making clothing for the poor as well as for the rich; probably more for the poor than for the rich, because the former will derive the greatest advantages from the cheapening of clothing thus produced. If he builds a railroad with it, that railroad will be employed in bringing hides from Texas to make shoes for the laborer's feet, or corn from Illinois for him to consume. The capitalist may or may not derive any benefit from it; but it is certain that the laborer will derive a benefit. If the capitalist builds a row of houses, the only use he can make of them is to get somebody to live in them. The amount of shelter that is available for laborers is thus increased, and they have just as much advantage of the houses while they live in them as if they owned them themselves; that is to say, as far as shelter is concerned, the house you live in is equally useful to you whether you own it or some one else owns it. But you say, perhaps, "The owner takes a tax from me in the shape of rent for living in it." This is true, and in the market this rent is the equivalent of the shelter; but it would not be the equivalent of the shelter if there were no capital to build houses at all. For every house which is burned down, and every house which is not built, the rent of the remaining ones is higher, while for every new house added the rent comes lower. However rents may vary, it is certain that if the number of houses is diminished from any cause whatever, there must be more people in one house, and thus more discomfort.

Again, what does the capitalist do with the money which you pay him for rent? Some part of it he may expend for his own exclusive benefit; but, as the world goes, the chances are that he puts the larger part of it into improvements which in some way benefit his fellow-men, laborers included. Some part of it goes to keep the very house in which you live in repair; another part, perhaps, to build new houses; another part to extend railroads, and so on. In all these ways, it is expended so as to increase the supply of food, clothing, and shelter available for the support of the laborer. Thus, all combinations among laborers to diminish or interfere with the development of capital amount to nothing but combinations to do the whole laboring class of the country, themselves included, as much harm as they can by interfering with the operation of the social system described in the first lesson.

We may now see that in spite of the antagonisms which from time to time arise between the employer and the employed, capital and labor are each indispensable to the other. How indispensable labor is to capital every one sees without argument, but many do not seem to see the other side of the truth. But this must be plain if you will reflect for a moment that every laborer or employé in the country is, under our present laws, perfectly at liberty to get along without the capitalist if he is able and willing to do so. If an engineer or fireman is dissatisfied with his wages, he is not compelled to remain and be oppressed; on the contrary, the whole world is before him where to choose. If a bricklayer or carpenter is not satisfied with what his employer pays him for his work, no law compels him to remain working for wages so low: he is free to build on his own account, and to combine with men in other trades to any extent to build houses for themselves. If the laborers of the country would combine in ever so feeble an effort to get along without the help of the capitalist, collecting all necessary capital for themselves, and working on their own account, they would at least show a laudable disposition to be independent. The very fact that they have never attempted this, and that during strikes they have remained idle, thus causing more suffering to themselves than to their employers, shows that the latter are really necessary to them.

One way in which the employer or capitalist is necessary to the laborer is this: when the two classes combine in any enterprise, say the building of a house, the former takes all the risk. Whether the house sells well or not, the men who build it get their wages, and thus are enabled to live, whereas it depends altogether on how the house sells whether the capitalist makes or loses. Thus, the men very wisely trade off their chances of large profit, which they might have if they built for themselves, for the sake of being certain of the means of living.

The best solution for these difficulties which so often arise between the two classes in question is to be found in some system of co-operation, whereby the laborer, besides having regular, but low wages, as a certainty, shall be allowed a share of the profits, if there are any. This plan has several times been tried, and always, I think, with success. If labor-unions generally would move for it, instead of waging a suicidal war by entirely refusing to work for weeks or months at a time, they would do more for their own well-being than by any other plan they have yet tried, and would show better than they ever have shown that they understood their own interests.

LESSON III.

STARVATION WAGES.

A FEW weeks ago it was said that several railroads of the country lowered the wages of their men to the starvation point. Now, I confess that I do not know what the "starvation point" is, and so cannot say whether this is true or not; but I will remark, in passing, that there has been within the past year or two a great fall in the price of nearly everything necessary to the laborer's comfort; and that starvation wages will buy a great deal more than they would two or three years ago. Possibly if the railroad employés had devoted half the exertion to getting cheap food and clothing which they have devoted to prevent a fall of wages, they would find that their starvation wages would secure them as many of the comforts of life as the higher wages of two or three years ago did. But we need not stop to discuss whether this is so or not. We must pass on to some further considerations. The men were not satisfied with their wages, and refused to run the trains. Now, if the reduction of the wages was really unnecessary and unjustifiable, the men were quite right in thus refusing to work, provided that they did not seek to interfere with the rights or with the property of any one else. But the fact was, that there were a large number of other men, whom we will call Jones, and Brown, and so on, quite ready to take the places of those who would not work, and to run the trains for those starvation wages. They had a perfect right thus to accept the best employment they could get, and the road had an equal right to employ them. But the strikers drove them off, refusing even to let them have this poor opportunity to earn a little to keep their families from starving. Now, what does this show? Why, the very fact that Brown and Jones were willing to enter the service of the roads at those starvation wages shows that they could not get even those wages at other employments. They were either absolutely out of employment, or were working for something below the limit which the companies set, or else they would not be willing to enter their service under the circumstances. Thus the strikers by their action prevented these unfortunate men from even earning the miserable pittance for which they themselves refused to work. You think, perhaps, that the companies ought not only to have paid higher wages to those who were actually running their trains, but also to have taken a number of these starving Joneses and Browns in, in order to help them. But the means of the companies are necessarily limited. A company gets only a certain number of dollars from passengers and freight with which to pay its employés, and it cannot pay out more than this amount for any purpose whatever, any more than two and two can make five.

We all know that the gross receipts of nearly every railway in the country have greatly diminished during the past five years. It is therefore simply impossible to run the roads without cutting down the wages of some one. The very fact that there were so many poor fellows ready to run the trains at the diminished wages, because there was nothing else for them to do, seems to me to prove that there was no entirely unjustifiable reduction. I confess I do not think those who wish for the improvement of the laboring class should have anything like as much sympathy with the strikers as they should have with those poor men unable to earn the pittance of perhaps ninety cents a day. In interfering with their employment, the strikers showed themselves in the light of cruel tyrants, regardless of those laws of freedom and property which have been the means of keeping them from serfdom.

I must not be understood as seeking to justify the general management of the railroads during the last ten years, or as claiming that the men had no reasonable ground of complaint. Every one who has the cause of humanity at heart must hope for the time when there will be more sympathy between the laborer and his employer, and when the latter will look on the former as one in whose happiness he has an interest. But improvements like this go on very, very slowly, so that no one generation can ever see them brought about, and any attempt to hurry them only keeps them back. Sympathy and good feeling are not promoted by war of any kind, and least of all by a war like that of the railroad men against law, order, and civilization generally. However bad railroad managers in general may be, in this particular case they were in the right and the others in the wrong.

There is one very important feature of strikes and labor movements generally which people seldom notice, but which should seriously modify our opinions of them. We are apt to think of all these movements as made for the benefit of the great masses of unskilled laborers, or, at least, as being planned and executed by them. A very little reflection upon facts which we all know will show us that this is an entire mistake, and that strikes of the most numerous class of laborers — the unskilled ones — are rare and unimportant. In the late railway war, it was not the men willing to work for ninety cents a day who struck, but engineers and firemen possessed of such skill that they could, in ordinary times, earn more than was sufficient for their support, and belonging to an association which was boasted to command millions of dollars. All the other strikes of which we have so often heard have been by miners, bricklayers, masons, carpenters, hatters, and so on, but not by day-laborers. Now, this last is the class which should most command the sympathy of the philanthropist, because it is the most helpless class; but it is the very one against which the rules and customs of trades-unions operate most vigorously. The higher classes can take care of themselves, but these cannot so easily do so.

The worst part of the policy of trades-unions is that which seeks to limit the number of men who shall be allowed to learn a trade. Not only are vast numbers of men thus compelled to remain day-laborers who might otherwise attain skill in some trade, but all the articles which skilled labor produces are made scarcer. If these articles were used only by men of wealth, the men who sympathize with the laborer would not so much care. But such is not the case. It is mathematically certain that laborers cannot have more house-room than they now have till more houses are built for them, and this cannot be done without more bricklayers, carpenters, plasterers, and so on. The same remark will apply to nearly everything which the laborer needs to live in comfort. Skilled labor is necessary to produce it, and many skilled laborers are banded together to make their work as scarce and dear as possible.

There is one important lesson to be learned from all this. The progress of humanity from the time when the laborer was little better than a serf, living in a smoky cabin with its thatched roof and unwholesome air, eating black bread, and going to his work barefoot, up to the present, when the industry of a continent is at work supplying his wants, has been very slow and gradual. This course of progress has always encountered enemies more or less effective. But the worst and most destructive enemy it has ever encountered is to be found in those trades-unions which have been engaged in saving up money from the laborers' earnings in order, from time to time, to wage wars against production through strikes. That a certain small proportion of these movements may have been justifiable I do not deny; but the larger number of them have been carried through at the expense of an amount of privation, misery, and even death, as well as of injury to the productive power of the country, for which no good trades-unions have ever done can compensate. However we may admire the heroism of the men engaged, we must not forget that their war has generally been waged against the very instrumentalities designed to feed, clothe, and shelter them.

To proceed further with these questions, we must know something of the nature and functions of *money*. Here we come into a field where it is almost as necessary to *unlearn* as it is to learn. There are two entirely groundless ideas prevalent respecting the value of money, which have no more real foundations than the notions about witchcraft which prevailed a couple of centuries ago, and on which a large part of the fallacies of the subject is founded. Until these ideas are, so to speak, unlearned, no progress is possible.

LESSON IV.

ONE DOLLAR.

THE first idea to which I allude is, that if anything is called a dollar by act of Congress, if every one passes and accepts it as a dollar, it must therefore have a definite and fixed value, and be for all practical purposes just as good as a gold dollar. You think, perhaps, that a dollar must be worth just one dollar, and neither more nor less; how, then, can its value be uncertain? I answer that two kinds of dollars can differ from each other in value just as much as two loaves of bread can in size and quality. You know very well, for instance, that during the past ten years our paper dollar has been worth from five to thirty per cent. less than the gold dollar. To explain the matter fully, I must perhaps be a little abstruse, and therefore ask a closer attention than I will elsewhere.

When I say that a paper dollar can have no definite and fixed value, I mean that it cannot be insured to buy you any fixed and definite quantity of the necessaries of life. Money has no value at all except for the things it will buy; you can neither eat it, drink it, nor wear it; nor can you even gain interest on it while it remains in your pocket. What you want of it is to buy things to eat, drink, and wear, and the number of these things it will buy, and not the number of dollars, is the measure of its value. You would not give a fig for a pocketful of dollars if you could buy only the half of a fig with them. If this year you had supported your family on five hundred dollars, but next year it should require one thousand dollars because, on the average, prices had doubled, people would say that the value of everything was twice as great as before. But this would be an incorrect use of language. Really the value of your dollars is only half what it was before. Please remember that this is the only sense in which I now use the word "value," and the only sense in which it has a definite practical meaning. Dollars and all other kinds of money are worth what they will buy you to eat and wear; and measuring value by any other standard is like trying to feed a hungry man on acts of Congress.

All the difficulty of this matter arises from the fact that *value* is something which cannot be seen nor felt. If Congress should enact that all the foot and yard measures of the country should be made of a kind of rubber which would shrink to nine inches in the course of a few months, but which were nevertheless stamped "One foot, by act of Congress," or "One yard," as the case might be, everybody would see at a glance how ridiculous it would be to require every one to buy and sell by such measures. If a man should boast of having grown a foot and a half in the course of a year, because last year he measured only five feet, while with the new india-rubber measures he was now six feet and a half by act of Congress, his neighbors would laugh at him. The fact that everybody might call the new rubber measures one foot, and might buy and sell by them, would not, in the view of any sensible man, make them as long as the old foot-rules.

The reason that these india-rubber measures would look so much more ridiculous than similar dollars is simply that their deficiency in length is obvious to the eye, whereas the depreciation of the dollar is not obvious. In reality, calling a thing one dollar, and legalizing it as such, no more makes it the equivalent of a gold dollar, or of anything else in value, than calling it a foot will make it a foot long, no matter what its real length may be. But we cannot see nor feel the depreciation of the dollar as we would see the shortening of the foot measure. We become aware of it only by the general rise of prices, and the general increase in the cost of living. This rise of prices, however, proves the depreciation in the same way that the little man measuring six feet six in his stockings would prove that the foot-rule with which he was measured was too short.

If, now, the reader will hereafter remember that "dollar" is only a word, not a thing; that calling a thing a dollar does not change its nature, and does not make it worth twenty-three grains of gold, any more than calling a piece of paper a horse, and having it declared and stamped a horse by act of Congress, would make it draw a carriage—if, I say, he will permanently remember this, he will have taken the first great step towards comprehending the financial question.

LESSON V.

VALUE CANNOT BE GIVEN BY GOVERNMENT.

THE second notion to be unlearned is intimately associated with the former one. It is that governments possess some wonderful power of giving value to money, which every one must admit, but which no one can explain. Widely as this notion is extended, it is as pure a superstition as was the old notion that a witch could make her enemy sick by secretly making a wax image of him, and then by sticking pins into it, roasting it before the fire, and otherwise torturing it, could make him suffer corresponding tortures. The disproof of this theory by an appeal to facts is easy and conclusive. Every man of intelligence knows that the coined money of all nations is worth only the gold which is in it, except that the coin bears a slight premium, owing to the certainty that it is the real metal; whereas the gold may have to be assayed, and the cost of the assay must be deducted from its value. In other words, the coined money may bear a premium over the mere bullion equal to the cost of coinage. The stamp of Government goes for absolutely nothing, except a certificate of the weight and quality of the metal.

Now, if the common notion were correct, the coin might be vastly more valuable than the crude bullion out of which it was made, the premium depending on how great and powerful a nation put its stamp on it. But all nations are here on a dead level; their stamps, one and all, go for just nothing, so far as giving value is concerned. The dollars of the poorest South American states, the sovereigns of England, the napoleons of France, and the gold bars fresh from the mines without any Government stamp upon them, all exchange in the markets of the world according to the amount of gold in them, and nothing else. This fact is a conclusive refutation of the opinion that Government can confer value on anything by its stamp.

A maxim is often quoted which is true in one sense and not true in another, but which people are expected to believe in the sense in which it is not true. It is said that the dollar is anything which the law makes it. To see in what sense this is true, let us take the similar, but easier, case of a loaf of bread. Our city authorities may have the power to declare how much bread shall constitute a loaf, and this year they may provide that the loaf shall weigh one pound; next year, two pounds; and the year after, half a pound. They might also, from time to time, allow the baker to add corn or rye meal to his flour. We might then say that the loaf of bread was anything which the law made it. But it would not follow that the loaf of one year was the same as that of another, and it would be monstrous for the law to suppose them the same. It is the same with the dollar. If Congress provides a gold dollar this year, and a silver dollar next year, and a paper dollar the year after, there is no necessary relation of value between these different dollars any more than between the loaves of bread we have supposed.

If, now, the reader will remember that there is only one kind of value, namely, that measured by the necessaries of life anything will command in the market, and that the value of a gold dollar does not differ in any essential respect from that of the same quantity of gold in a nugget, he will have taken the second great step towards understanding the money question.

LESSON VI.

THE VALUE OF PAPER MONEY.

WITH these two ideas unlearned, we are in a proper state of mind to inquire what gives value to paper money. You know that, practically, far the greater part of the business of the world is carried on by using paper or credit instead of gold. Only an insignificant fraction of mercantile payments are made by actually counting out gold. If one merchant has to pay another a thousand dollars in gold, he simply hands him a check for the amount, which the second merchant, perhaps, passes over to some one else. Here is a piece of paper, of no value whatever in itself, passed from hand to hand just as if its value were a thousand gold dollars. How is this? Can we say with correctness that the check has any real value? The answer is clear and simple. The value does not reside in the check itself, but in the 23,200 grains (say three pounds avoirdupois) of gold to which the holder of the check is entitled, and which he knows the bank is able and ready to pay him. That is all. If the bank is not bound to pay the check, no matter how many dollars may be marked on it, no matter how beautiful the engraving, it is worth nothing. If the check is not payable in gold, but in greenbacks, then it is worth not a thousand dollars in gold, but only in greenbacks. So it is with all the commercial paper money of the world, which circulates in such enormous quantities in place of money. Its sole basis is that responsible men are bound to pay it, and its only value depends upon the weight of the gold to which it entitles the holder, no matter whether it is called pounds, francs, or dollars.

Observe carefully that it is not sufficient that the paper "represents" so much gold, or that the firm which issues it is very wealthy or powerful. The holder of the paper must have an acknowledged right to the gold, which the bank is not going to dispute. If there is any doubt whether he himself, or any one to whom he may pass the check, will be able to get the gold for it, then the check will be depreciated. If it is certain that no one can ever get the gold for it, its value will be just that of a pretty picture for the children to play with, no matter how strongly it may be declared to represent a thousand dollars.

Now, with a single exception, which we shall consider presently, the value of Government paper money is determined in precisely the same way with that of mercantile paper. In itself it has no value at all. Congress may stamp it one dollar or one hundred dollars; but unless it entitles the owner to claim something, it is a mere piece of paper. If the owner can actually get a gold dollar with it, it is worth a gold dollar; otherwise it will be more or less depreciated in value, according to the hope of future payment which the holders may entertain. Of course Congress can make every one call it a dollar and receive it under that name, but we have seen in the first lesson that this does not give it real value —that is, purchasing power. If any one is compelled to take it, he simply puts up the

price of everything he has to sell in proportion to the depreciation of the paper, so that the result is the same as if the paper passed at a discount.

We must now point out a fallacy by which the supporters of irredeemable paper money often try to get round these considerations. It is said that the greenbacks, or their proposed paper dollars, are to be issued "on the credit of the nation," and therefore must have value in proportion to that credit, even if the nation does not redeem them.

The word "credit" is here used in some peculiar sense (which no one can fully explain) wholly different from its commercial sense. In the world of business, "credit" includes the ability and the obligation to pay all demands in cash as they become due. A man or a firm that cannot do this has no credit, however excellent it may be in other respects. Suppose you should be travelling in a distant city, and, going to the cashier of your hotel for change, he hands you a ten-dollar bill on the banking firm of Spread, Brothers, & Co.

"Are you sure this bill is good?" you inquire.

"Good as gold, sir. The firm of Spread, Brothers, & Co. is the greatest in this State, possessed of unbounded wealth, and its operations extend over the whole globe."

"Then," you reply, "I suppose if I take this bill to their counter, they will pay it?"

"Pay it! Why, no, sir. You would be hooted by the small boys in the street, and laughed at by Spread's clerks. The credit of the firm is so excellent, and all its debts so well secured by real estate and bonds worth millions of dollars, that both the firm and the community concluded, ten or twelve years ago, that there was not the slightest need of their redeeming their bills, and they are never going to do it."

"I don't understand that kind of credit. In my State, credit paper is something which the party issuing is bound to pay when required; and if he does not pay, he has no credit, no matter how rich he is."

"Of course twopenny firms must pay. But we claim that a firm so great, powerful, and wealthy as that of Mr. Spread need not pay."

"Well, sir," you would reply, "I don't see what difference it makes to me how wealthy Spread's firm is, or how well their paper is secured, if I can't get any of their wealth in exchange for my bill. I always thought the advantage of having the paper of a wealthy firm was that it was surer to be paid; but if the richer the firm, the less the need of paying, I would rather have the bill of some smaller house."

"Ah, you know nothing about finance, I see; and I'll get you some foreign money rather than argue further with you."

If a hotel cashier should talk in this way to you, you would be a little puzzled to say whether he was joking or in earnest. And yet great statesmen do argue in just that way about our greenbacks. There are bills to the amount of four hundred millions of dollars afloat, reading, "*The United States will pay the bearer —— dollars.*" Yet if you should take one of these bills to the Government's counter, asking that this promise be redeemed, the clerks would laugh at you. A year or two since some one did this very thing, and the newspapers speculated on the man's sanity, while a Treasury official thought he was only trying to make himself notorious. If a politician tries to justify permanent non-payment, he will talk about the credit and wealth of the nation exactly as the hotel clerk talked about Spread, Brothers, & Co. Now, it will be a very profitable mental exercise if the reader will ask himself what is meant by the promise, "*The United Sates will pay the bearer —— dollars;*" and if, also, for each theory of the subject he may form, he will consider how it will look for a banking firm to put that same interpretation on its promises. To give the reader time to think this matter over, I will here close this lesson.

LESSON VII.

WHY HAS THE GREENBACK ANY VALUE?

In the last two lessons I have sought to show the fallacy of the various notions afloat that Government possesses some peculiar power of giving value to coined money or stamped paper. The reader who has informed himself on financial history will be familiar with many illustrations of the unpleasant truth of the views here maintained. In the history of the bills of credit which used to be issued by our colonies, and which have been issued by other governments in difficulties, the story has been told over and over again. But there are also some apparent exceptions—cases in which money, though for a greater or less space of time not redeemable, has not depreciated to nothing. Our greenbacks are a case in point. The reader may say, "On your theory greenbacks are mere pieces of paper, and ought not to be worth more than the paper on which they are printed.

How do you explain the fact that they continue worth from eighty-five to ninety cents on the dollar in gold?"

I answer that there are two reasons for the continued value of the greenback. The first is, that everything which circulates as money in a community may have a certain value merely in virtue of its usefulness as currency. Even the value of gold is much greater than it would be but for its usefulness as money. There are certain conditions under which it is theoretically possible for unredeemed bills to be on a par with gold. These conditions, which it is very important to bear in mind, are:

1. *That they shall actually pass current, and be received as "bankable funds."*

2. *That their quantity shall be so small that they are insufficient to form the entire circulating medium, so that some gold has still to be used. The universal experience of all nations and people who have ever tried it is, that as soon as the currency is issued in such quantities as entirely to displace gold, it begins to depreciate—that is, gold is at a premium.*

This is the secret of the non-depreciation

of the bills of the Bank of France during the last few years, while specie payments were suspended. There were not enough notes in Paris to transact its business, so that gold had constantly to be used in part. Had the American theory of plenty of currency been acted on, there is no knowing what would have been the result.

Now, although our greenbacks have been issued in a greater amount than was necessary for business, as is conclusively proved by their depreciation, yet the amount has been limited by law. It has been still further limited by the fact that the revenues of the Government have exceeded its expenditures, so that a large quantity of the greenbacks have not been in actual circulation. And so long as the total issue of greenbacks is strictly limited to its present amount, there is no danger of their total loss of value.

The second reason for the value of the greenback is, that there has been more or less expectation of its being redeemed sometime within the life of the present generation. Though no one has seen exactly how specie payments were going to be brought about, the general business sentiment of the country has been that we must reach them in some way. The greenbacks have always been counted as part of the public debt, which proceeding implies an obligation to redeem. In order to set at rest all doubt on this matter, Congress, in 1869, passed a law pledging the faith of the nation to the payment of the greenbacks in coin; and, in 1875, it set a date (January 1st, 1879) when this payment should commence.

To these two reasons, and to no others, are we to attribute the fact that our greenbacks have not gone the way of all previous systems of irredeemable paper money. The reader must carefully notice that neither of these reasons is based on the fact that the greenbacks are issued by a great government. The unredeemed paper of France was issued, not by the Government, but by a bank; yet, as we have seen, it was more successful than our Government paper. It is not the party which issues, but its *quantity*, and the *prospect of its redemp-*

tion, which determine its value. Indeed, bank paper is, under such circumstances, far less liable to depreciation than Government paper, for the reason that, if the public is determined, the bank can always be made to pay up, while the Government cannot. The case is just like your preference for the paper of a small house, which must pay, over that of a firm so rich and powerful that it is above paying.

You see at once that if the policy of the inflationists were permanently inaugurated, both of the reasons for the value of the greenback would be knocked from under it, and it would rapidly go the way of the Continental currency, and every other system of Government paper money that has ever been tried. With no intention to redeem in coin, a note would be a mere piece of paper; and if issued in such quantities as would be demanded, although every one might call them "dollars," their purchasing power would diminish without limit.

LESSON VIII.

THE 3.65-BOND PLAN.

Some advocates of paper money have a more or less dim perception of the fact that a paper currency, to have real value, must be redeemable in something. At the same time they are conscious that paying out solid gold is a very disagreeable thing to be obliged to do. So they have a most ingenious plan for redeeming the currency in something vastly better than gold, and which will cost the Government nothing but the trouble of printing it. This something is to be Government bonds bearing interest at the rate of 3.65 per cent., both principal and interest being payable in the same paper, to redeem which the bonds are issued.

Now, I must say at the outset that if the principal and interest of these bonds were payable in gold, and if the rate of interest were so high that capitalists would be ready to invest in them—if, say, it were five, or even four and one-half, per cent.—there would be nothing absurd in the plan. It would, indeed, be subject to the fatal objection that the currency of the whole country would be liable to suffer from any political crisis which might prevent the payment of interest on the bonds, but even then the currency would be in no worse predicament than it is now.

But when it is proposed that both principal and interest shall be payable in the very currency to redeem which the bonds are issued, it is very hard to approach the subject with due gravity. Look at it a moment. You have your pocketful of greenbacks, each promising to pay you so many dollars. You take them to the Treasury, and ask them to be paid. You receive in return a bond, promising "*United States will pay the bearer —— dollars, with interest at* 3.65 *per cent. per annum.*" You go for your interest, and you receive greenbacks: "*United States will pay the bearer —— dollars.*" You ask for your principal, and you receive the very same old formula. Nothing are you ever to get but paper stamped,

"*United States will pay the bearer —— dollars.*" You can only choose between promises with interest and promises without interest *ad infinitum*, the interest, you must remember, being also payable in promises.

What real value could such currency and such bonds have? As we have already seen, the value of bonds and notes of every kind is measured by that of the money in which they are to be paid. A bond payable in pounds sterling is worth more than one payable in the same number of dollars, because the pound is worth more than the dollar. A bond payable in gold dollars is worth more than one payable in paper dollars, in the proportion that gold is worth more than paper. The bonds being payable in paper, we cannot tell the value of them until we know the value of the paper in which they are to be paid. But we find that the value of the paper depends entirely on that of the bonds, because the notes are payable in nothing but bonds. You can exchange notes for bonds, and *vice versa*, as long as you please, but can never measure the value of either except by trying how much bread and meat it will buy in the market.

The principles on which this ingenious system of finance are based need not be confined to money; they can also be applied to navigation, so as to prevent shipwrecks. A ship's anchor frequently fails to hold her in a storm, and she may thus be driven on a lee shore. Scores of vessels are wrecked in this way every year. The new plan of anchoring, which is open to the world, is this: dispense with all such uncertain things as anchors, and send your ships out in pairs. Then, whenever your two ships—the *Eagle* and the *Ocean Wave*—are in danger of being blown on a lee shore in a gale of wind, lash the *Eagle* firmly to the *Ocean Wave*, so that the wind can't move her an inch. Then, lash the *Ocean Wave* firmly to the *Eagle*, so that she cannot move either. Then the two ships will bid defiance to the storm, and their crews will look on calmly as they see those unwise captains who trust in anchors drifting by them. You see the principles involved. The *Eagle* is the greenback, the *Ocean Wave* the bond.

The greenback is based on the bond, as the *Eagle* is lashed to the *Ocean Wave*. The bond is based on the greenback, as the *Ocean Wave* is lashed to the *Eagle*. And thus we have in navigation, as in finance, a "subtle principle," which will regulate the movement of finance and of ships "as accurately as the motion of the steam-engine is regulated by its governor."

There is still another point of view from which it is worth while to look at this important question. We have already had occasion to mention the fact, which every one of intelligence knows, that the money of all the world exchanges exactly according to the weight of gold in it, and according to no other standard. The pound sterling, for instance, exchanges for about four dollars and eighty-five cents in gold, not because either Congress or the British Government ever agreed just what the relative value should be, but because there is as much gold in one pound as in four dollars and eighty-five cents. Our gold dollar, again, is worth four German marks, because it contains that many times the quantity of gold. But on the new system of finance we are to ignore the gold basis entirely, and our paper dollar is to have absolutely nothing in common with the gold dollar except the name. Does it seem to you that this paper dollar, which has nothing to do with gold, should be worth twenty-three grains of gold just because in former generations we used to put that much gold in a coin of the same name? You might as well think that if Congress would only stamp a piece of paper "*This is a loaf of bread*," you could eat and digest it. The fact is, there is no more reason why it should buy twenty-three grains of gold in the markets of the world than ten grains or one grain. Its purchasing power might begin with fifteen or twenty grains, but it would be sure to sink from year to year to no one knows where.

Some may say, What difference does it make to me how much gold a dollar will buy? Let those who want gold pay the market-price for it. I answer that we are to consider not merely the quantity of gold which the paper dollar will buy, but the quantity of flour, beef, and shoes. Would you feel perfectly safe in binding yourself to give forty pounds of flour or three hours' work, a year hence, to any one who would agree to give you in exchange a piece of paper stamped "One Dollar" by act of Congress? If you are prudent, you certainly would not.

LESSON IX.

THE MYSTERY OF MONEY.

When, in the early years of the greenbacks, our statesmen saw gold going up in the market, and wished to explain it without supposing a depreciation of the dollar, they coined a word to express their view of the matter, and said gold was "demonetized," and turned into a mere article of traffic, like leather and iron. I allude to this notion because it is based on a very common fallacy which underlies many of our notions about money. This fallacy consists in supposing that by being used as a medium of exchange gold becomes *mone-*

tized, and thereby is affected with some mysterious power as a measure of value. We see this fallacy in the importance sometimes attached to the question what is and what is not money, the idea being that if a thing is money it is very different from what it would be if it were not money. In fact, however, anything is money which people universally give and take in exchange for their labor or merchandise. Salt, cattle, and iron have been used as such. In our colonial times, tobacco was used for money, and clumsy though it was, it was far better money than the bills of credit the States used to issue with such disastrous effects. Its use as money did not in any way change its nature, its properties, or even its real value. As men advance in civilization they find that these clumsy things will no longer answer, and take to gold and silver. The advantages of the precious metals are: (1) they include a great value in a small space; (2) they are not liable to decay or other damage from keeping; (3) they can be divided up into small and definite portions.

Gold in its crude state, entirely uncoined, was very recently in use as money in some parts of California and Mexico. But the difficulty of being sure of the weight and quality of the metal is a serious evil in such cases; so at a very early stage in civilization governments step in and coin the gold. Coinage, as we have already explained, has no other value than that of a certificate of the quantity and fineness of the gold in the coin.

Thus far there is no mystery. A coin is simply so much gold or silver, which people pass from hand to hand as the Indians used to pass wampum, and the colonists tobacco. The next step is the use of credit paper. In any mercantile community it would soon be found that there was no need of actually counting out the coin for every payment, and that trouble and danger of loss would be avoided by keeping the gold in a bank, and paying over checks or bills entitling the holder to so much gold at the bank. As every owner of a check could go to the bank and get the gold if he wanted it, they are just as valuable as the gold itself. We might thus imagine all the money of a community kept in one bank, and all payments made by checks on the bank. The gold would then lie there in the vaults year after year, disturbed only when some one required it, from time to time, to send away, or to melt into some useful article. The bank would also have to be paid for the expense of keeping the gold and paying the checks. To avoid this, the modern banking system is introduced, by which the bank is allowed to loan part of the gold out at interest for short periods, and thus compensate itself by the interest it receives. It still holds itself responsible to pay every one who wants it his gold on demand; and as long as the confidence of the business community is maintained, it can do this with perfect safety. It may have credits out, payable on demand, to three or four times the amount of gold in its vaults; but, unless an extraordinary number of depositors should rush after their gold at once, all demands can be satisfied. Unless a panic occurs, there is no more danger of this than of every one wearing out his shoes at once, and besieging the shoe-stores on the same day for a new pair. Even then the worst that can happen to the holder of the note is having to wait a few days for his money.

Such is the history of money, in brief. It is simply a commodity like gold, or a paper certificate entitling the holder to a commodity. Seeing these paper certificates pass from hand to hand, with only one man in a hundred going to get the gold to which they entitle him, people of wild ideas are constantly jumping to the conclusion that they need not entitle the holder to anything, and that a stage of progress may be reached in which mere stamped paper will answer the purpose of money. The plans for attaining this end are as numerous and as chimerical as those for attaining perpetual motion. One might with equal reason claim that the human race would reach a state of things in which such gross food as bread and beef would no longer be necessary, and people would live entirely on ideas.

LESSON X.

THE EVIL OF A DEPRECIATING CURRENCY.

AT this stage the reader may ask, What harm if the currency does depreciate? What difference whether it takes two or two dozen paper dollars to buy a pair of shoes, so long as they pass current? To answer this question fully would require me to write a large book. The history of mankind for the last two centuries is full of examples showing that a depreciating currency is the greatest source of injury to the business of a nation, being nothing less than a national calamity. A brief summary of the most obvious evils is all we now have time for.

1. People are constantly bargaining for the sale of their goods or their services in exchange for a certain number of dollars, to be paid them at some future time. Salaried men and laborers engage themselves by the day, the month, or the year. Economical people put money in the savings-

bank, to be repaid, perhaps, at the end of many years. All these arrangements are made under the belief that the dollars you are going to receive will buy you, on the average, as many of the means of living as they will now. If you are to be paid in gold dollars, you may be morally certain that your expectations in this respect will be fulfilled, because the experience of mankind in all ages has shown that the purchasing power of gold is never subject to great and rapid fluctuations. But if you are to be paid in paper dollars, no man knows what they will buy. The laborer will find, week after week, that prices rise so fast, his wages will buy less and less for his family. If the policy is once adopted to issue all the paper dollars that may be required by commerce, it is not only possible, but highly probable, that thirty of them would not, twenty years hence, buy a decent meal. See scale of prices in Hayti, for example, where this policy has been adopted. What does the proposed paper-money bond amount to? It will say that the United States will pay the bearer one hundred dollars. What does this mean, on the new plan? Simply this:

On demand the United States promises to print and stamp for the bearer one hundred paper dollars, and does hereby guarantee that the said papers shall be called dollars everywhere in this country.

If the United States also guaranteed that these dollars should buy some specified portion of the necessaries of life — forty pounds of flour, or eight pounds of beef, for example—the promise might amount to something. But when all reason and all experience show that the paper dollars will probably lose nearly all power of purchasing, who will agree to take them? Is it right for the Government to adopt a policy which will end in the bitter deception of all its citizens who do not know the difference between gold and paper dollars?

2. The second evil of depreciating paper is, that it necessarily enriches speculators at the expense of the rest of the community. The sharp speculator is no theorist. He knows exactly what the effect of depreciating paper is, and takes advantage

of it. He buys goods on credit, and holds them until their prices rise, then sells them, and pays off his debt with a part of the proceeds, pocketing the balance as profits of the operation. Of course great business activity is thus produced. The manufacturer hires operatives at present prices, well knowing that the goods they produce will rise on his hands so as to yield him a handsome profit. The operatives receive their pay in depreciated dollars, and are the real sufferers.

3. The third evil is, that extravagance is fostered. Sudden fortunes are made by speculation, while no one really feels any poorer. The salaried man finds it hard to make both ends meet; but, as he gets his usual income, he must not complain of the high prices. Property of all kinds rising in price, property-holders are at first very much pleased. They do not clearly see that the rise is due to the fact that the dollars by which the value is estimated are worth less than before. They are much in the position of a man who, having a handful of gold dollars, should be furnished

with a pair of spectacles which made every dollar look like an eagle, and who, therefore, thinks he has suddenly increased his wealth ten times. If he is a good-hearted man, he spends some of his surplus in giving a feast to all his friends, and this is done by so many that we have almost an era of extravagance. Of course the extravagance has to be bitterly paid for.

4. The fourth evil of depreciating currency is, that it aggravates the very evil which it is designed to prevent, not only by making the rate of interest high, but by making it almost impossible to borrow money on any terms whatever. This may seem paradoxical, but it is a fact well proved by the bitter experience of those unfortunate people who have been attracted by the song of the paper-money siren. There are two reasons for this effect. One is, that, owing to the enormous nominal prices to which all goods mount under a system of depreciated paper money, more money is required to transact the business of the country just in proportion as more

is issued. When everything costs twice what it now does, you must take twice as much money in your pocket when you go on a journey or make a purchase; and you would, from this cause alone, find money just as scarce as before. If your wife wants two or three hundred dollars every time she goes shopping, you need a large pile of money. But the principal reason is, that the constant rise in prices stimulates borrowing for the purpose of speculation, as just explained. When a large number of people are anxious to borrow all the money that can be had, and willing to pay a high rate of interest for it, money to borrow must be scarce. When every one is anxious to buy, and wants to borrow all the money he can get to buy with, a competition must send up the rate of interest.

All this is little more than history in brief. If the reader requires further details, he must read the financial history of the French Revolution, of the American colonies, of our own Revolution, and of business and gold speculation during the early years of our civil war. Indeed, I can hardly conceive of a reasonable man reading these histories, and remaining a believer in irredeemable paper money, any more than I can conceive of his wanting to drive across a ricketty bridge after knowing that every heavy vehicle which ever tried to cross it had fallen through and been destroyed. As very few of my readers will have time to consult these histories, I shall try, in a subsequent lesson, to give an idea of what they are. To those who desire to inform themselves farther, I commend such books as Gouge's "Short History of Paper Money and Banking in the United States," Sumner's "History of American Currency," and the financial chapters of Thiers's "History of the French Revolution."

When reason and history unite in showing such serious evils as the result of depreciating currency, and no fruits but such as turn to bitter ashes in the mouth, what shall we say to those ignorant or visionary men who promise a millennium under a paper-money system, telling you that there shall be no more panics and no more scarcity of money?

LESSON XI.

A FEW FACTS.

It is very common, in discussions of subjects like this, to call for "facts," many people thinking that a single fact is worth bushels of reasoning. Whether this opinion is well or ill founded, there is nothing which the advocates of inflation so carefully conceal as the well-known facts of the history of money. Wendell Phillips, for instance, is credited with saying that specie payments mean specie when you do not want it, and nothing but paper when you do. No better illustration of the wildness with which such men talk can be given than merely putting this statement alongside of facts. These facts are such as no inflationist will have the hardihood to deny, however much he may try to explain them away, and they are worthy of being carefully borne in mind.

First Fact.—For fifty years past there has not been a day when an owner of an English bank-note could not get it paid in gold, nor is it likely that such a day will be seen for five hundred years to come. Nor has there, in all probability, been a business day at the banks when one or more persons, and generally dozens or hundreds of them, did not want gold. Hardly a business day now passes in which the Bank of England does not pay out gold to the amount of tens or even hundreds of thousands of dollars, to people wanting it. Remember this when you read or hear that specie payments cannot be kept up on the limited supply of gold now available. In thus talking as if there were some great difficulty in keeping paper always redeemable, and as if a suspension every twenty years was a matter of course, people bear in mind only the experience of our comparatively weak banks, and do not look at the reason of the thing. In the fact that the Bank of England has never suspended specie payment, or thought of suspending, for a day since 1822, we have an example much more worthy of imitation. Having gone on so successfully for two entire generations, the governors of that institution would now almost as soon think of committing suicide as of suspending.

Second Fact.—Under this policy of constant adherence to specie redemption, the little island of Great Britain has maintained the commercial supremacy of the world. London has become its great monetary centre, and, in spite of her system of land tenure and other institutions which tend to the disadvantage of her poorer classes, the average laborer of England is better off than that of any other country in Europe.

Third Fact.—There is no case recorded in history of a government issuing paper money not redeemable in gold or silver, and in quantities sufficient for commerce, without that paper money depreciating. The cases of such attempts and of their failure are so numerous that a whole volume of history would be required to recount them.

Fourth Fact.—There is now twice as much paper currency per capita of our population as during the six years preceding our civil war. Between 1854 and 1861, the total bank circulation averaged between one hundred and ninety and two hundred millions. Now, including our legal tenders and national bank-notes, it is not far from six hundred millions. Without aiming at any useless refinement in numbers, we may say, in a general way, that we have now 50 per cent. more population, and three times as much paper currency, as between 1854 and 1861. Therefore, it cannot be from any want of currency that we are suffering.

If you tell these facts to an inflationist, he may denounce them vigorously, and complain that you remember them, and say they have nothing to do with present questions; but he will not dare to deny them unless he cares nothing for truth. There is, however, one deception against which you must be on your guard. The Government of England has, on several occasions, when there was a great pressure for money in London, "suspended," temporarily, a certain clause in the banking law which prohibits the Bank of England from issuing notes when its supply of specie falls below a certain limit, and a class of inflationists frequently try to deceive those of their hearers who are not acquainted with financial history by talking as if this were a suspension of specie payment. Really, this suspension is only a *permission* to issue notes, of which the Bank would not think of availing itself, if there were any serious danger of having to refuse their redemption.

LESSON XII.

THE LESSONS OF HISTORY.

To compress anything like a history into a single chapter is, indeed, extremely difficult. Still, there are certain general and universal features in the history of paper money, both in this and other countries, which are too instructive to be neglected. To understand what those features are, we must revert to some ideas set forth in Lesson IV., viz., that the words "dollar," "pound," etc., are mere names of some tangible thing; and that if the things to which those names attach differ from each other, the fact that they are called by the same name does not give them any common value. It is said that in one period of Roman history the Gauls had to pay a certain monthly tribute to the Romans, and that one of the governors of Gaul ordered that the year should be divided into fourteen months, in order that the Gauls should thus be compelled to pay a greater amount of tribute in the course of a year. The meaning of the words in a contract was thus altered after the contract had been made, in order that it might mean something different from what the parties originally intended. This kind of legal fraud is so obvious, and so repulsive to every sentiment of honor in the mind of man, that it can never be practised except when the alteration in the meaning of words is not apparent. The only case in which people can be readily imposed on by such alteration is that of money; and the great feature of the history of money, especially paper money, to which I wish to call attention, is the manner in which words expressing value, such as "dollar," "shilling," "pound," "florin," "mark," etc., were made to express different degrees of real value at different times, in order to meet the supposed exigencies of the hour.

We scarcely know when this kind of fraud began. It is said that the Roman Emperor Elagabalus, being entitled to receive annually from his subjects a certain number of pieces of gold, each of which pieces was called an *aureus*, cunningly increased the amount of gold in this coin so that they had to pay him more than they bargained for. The history of England in its earlier stages affords many instances in which the cheat was in the opposite direction. It has been no new thing, when a king of England found himself heavily in debt, to diminish the amount of silver in the pound sterling, in order that the debt might be more easily discharged. From the Norman Conquest until the reign of Edward the Third, the pound sterling contained a pound of silver. It has now less than one-third of its original value; that is, a pound silver is now worth more than three pounds sterling. In Scotland the practice was carried still farther. The house of Stuart, in a century and a half, reduced the quantity of silver in the pound to less than one-twentieth of its original amount. This kind of fraud was just as mean as if the kings had owed their subjects a certain number of yards of cloth, and had then by royal decree made a yard-measure shorter, in order that they might more easily discharge their debts.

In the times which we have described, paper money was almost unknown. A few centuries ago it was gradually discovered by bankers that a bill of credit in any form whatever, entitling the holder to a certain amount of gold in a bank, would pass from hand to hand as money just as readily as the coin itself. As this sort of currency had some advantages over gold, and could be made profitable to the bankers, the paper-money system of the present time was gradually introduced into nearly all civilized countries. Then arose the delusion, the exposure of which is one of the objects of these lessons, viz., that because these pieces of paper passed from hand to hand without being immediately returned to the bank for the gold to which they entitled the bearer, it was not necessary that they should entitle the bearer to anything. It was thought that if the Government would only declare these papers to be themselves pounds, florins, dollars, marks, piastres, etc., they would be just as valuable, and would take the place of these several coins. A regard for common-sense and honesty has, however, prevented this policy from being carried out except under two conditions. One of these conditions is that of such gross ignorance of political economy on the part of the public that they think there must be some real connection between the value of these pieces of paper and that of the coins called by the same name. The other condition is that of the Government failing to collect sufficient revenue to meet its expenses, and thus being driven to pay these expenses by issuing paper money to its creditors. A Government having the power to make its issues a legal tender can get along for a while without revenue by paying its expenses in this kind of money; and if the Government is a weak one, engaged in war, the temptation to this policy is especially strong.

Among our earliest colonists, the first of these conditions was completely fulfilled. To say that they knew nothing of political economy is not a reproach to them, because such a science did not then exist. The delusion that value depended in some way upon the stamp or word of the Government, and not on the desire of men to possess useful things, had a strong hold on the minds of men everywhere. There was so little specie in the colonies that a resort to some substitute seemed an absolute necessity; and the most convenient substitute of all was the issue of bills of credit by the several colonial governments, because these bills cost the governments nothing but the expense of printing, and could be used to pay out to the public creditors. Ingenious as are the projects now afloat for the issue of paper money, I do not believe there is one which you will not find to have been tried during those times, and to have proved a total failure. The amount of money afloat was increased and diminished without any regard to the wants of commerce, and thus the most disastrous fluctuations in its value were produced; so that no one who had to pay a debt of five pounds could say, two or three years in advance, what the value of the pounds would be at that time. Our colonists tried notes with interest, and notes without interest; notes issued to pay their expenses, and notes issued as a loan on security; but the result was always the same. The more they were issued, the more they were depreciated, the measure of this depreciation being the rise in the price of silver. As they depreciated, they drove what little silver currency there was from the colonies, and it did not return until the notes were withdrawn.

The most well known of these paper-money systems was that of the Continental Congress, known as "Continental money." The first issue of these notes, to the amount of six millions, was made in 1775. They were, perhaps, the nearest approach on record to the ideal paper money for which our greenback friends are now wishing. They were, in fact, simple certificates that the bearer thereof was entitled to a certain number of Spanish milled dollars, without any statement as to when or how he was ever going to get these dollars. They bore no interest; they were not convertible into coin or any kind of bonds; they were not secured by anything at all. The only point in which they failed to conform to the ideal greenback of the future was, that instead of being declared "dollars" pure and simple, the words "Spanish milled dollars" were used. After the issue exceeded a certain limit, the inevitable process of depreciation commenced. It continued slowly, but regularly, throughout the whole Revolutionary War. Every fall in the value of the paper necessitated larger and larger issues, until, finally, two hundred millions of it were in circulation, and all hope of redemption vanished. It might have been supposed that when the war closed, and the power which issued it became a recognized independent nation, its value would increase; but such was not the case. Instead of increasing, it became so completely worthless that it no longer served the purpose even of money, but had to be completely thrown aside, and replaced by silver coin and issues based upon coin.

The worst feature of this issue was not, however, its depreciation, nor its final disappearance from commerce; but the premium which it offered to speculators who foresaw what was coming. Keen-sighted men, knowing the result of this continual issue of paper money, saw very well that the prices of all commodities, especially those which were necessary to carry on military operations, would inevitably rise. Accordingly, it became good policy for these men to invest all the money they could earn or borrow in food and clothing, and to hold on to this food and clothing until the price should rise. For instance, suppose that flour was now ten dollars a barrel. A man borrows a thousand dollars from his patriotic neighbor, and with it buys a hundred barrels of flour. He keeps this flour a year, and the price having doubled in the mean while, or, to speak more exactly, the dollars he has to pay being only worth half as much as they were when he borrowed them, he can sell out half of his flour for money enough to pay his whole debt, and can keep the other half as a clear profit on the operation. We had an experience very similar to this in the earlier years of our Civil War, when gold speculators, foreseeing the depreciation of the Government currency, made their fortunes by buying gold on time. Returning to the Revolutionary period, many of my readers may remember the complaint of Washington of the great injury done the country by the "forestallers," as these speculators were called, and his wish that they could all be hanged. Such complaints were very natural, but they were simply complaints of what, taking human nature as it is, were the inevitable results of the financial policy pursued by the Government.

When the Constitution of the United States was framed, the members of the

Convention met together with the experience of more than a century of paper money weighing upon their minds. They saw innumerable evils without any good to counterbalance them. Every argument for the alluring cause of the evil had been refuted by the bitter test of experience. They thought that one of the greatest boons they could bestow upon their posterity would be that of making this crying source of national evil impossible. Accordingly, they introduced a provision absolutely prohibiting the States from ever issuing bills of credit. As no power to issue such bills was given to the United States, they no doubt supposed that in doing this they had forever relieved the country from the greatest source of financial trouble with which it had ever been afflicted. This provision of the Constitution was deemed so important by Judge Story that we shall quote his words, and those of the *Federalist*, to show the views of the subject taken by those who spoke more directly from experience than we do:

"The prohibition to emit bills of credit

cannot, perhaps, be more forcibly vindicated than by quoting the glowing language of the *Federalist*, a language justified by that of almost every contemporary writer, and attested in its truth by facts from which the mind almost involuntarily turns away at once with disgust and indignation. 'This prohibition,' says the *Federalist*, 'must give pleasure to every citizen in proportion to his love of justice and his knowledge of the true springs of public prosperity. The loss which America has sustained since the peace from the pestilent effects of paper money on the necessary confidence between man and man, on the necessary confidence in the public councils, on the industry and morals of the people, and on the character of republican government, constitutes an enormous debt against the States chargeable with this unadvised measure which must long remain unsatisfied, or, rather, an accumulation of guilt which can be expiated no otherwise than by a voluntary sacrifice on the altar of justice of the power which has been the instrument of it.'

"It was the object of the prohibition to cut up the whole mischief by the roots, because it had been deeply felt throughout all the States, and had deeply affected the prosperity of all."

So great a reform as the prohibition of irredeemable paper could not, however, be inaugurated all at once, any more than a country could become civilized in a single generation. The evil which it was sought to blot out forever has always reappeared from time to time, in a milder form, it is true, but one which is still an evil, namely, over-issues of bank-notes.

The story of our bank-notes is very much of the same general nature with that of our colonial money, only not so bad. In times when business is brisk, when everybody is happy, and when speculation is rife, the banks would issue paper, and discount the notes of merchants to an unusual extent. What little specie there was in the country would then, in great part, leave it; and after a while the inevitable crash would come. The banks would be compelled at the same time to suspend specie payments, and to contract their issues. Speculators would be unable to meet their engagements, and a general fall of prices would result, accompanied with great distress among the laboring classes. The most notable case of this, a case which every one of my readers either remembers or has heard of, is that of the great crash of 1837. We are just finishing up a similar experience at the present time. The enormous issue of paper money by our Government and our national banks during the Civil War is now followed by precisely the same consequences which have followed every previous issue recorded in history.

In our own case, it is remarkable that the depression and crash have come before the withdrawal of the paper money. We have still in circulation nearly all the greenbacks and all the national-bank notes ever authorized; and yet the general distress and depression of business could not have been greater if they had all been absolutely withdrawn from circulation, and people had been left to get a new currency as best they could.

The French, during the earlier years of their Revolution, had an experience not dissimilar to our own. The national expenses were so much in excess of the revenues of that nation, that it was determined to issue bills of credit known as assignats. These bills bore a greater resemblance to some of our earlier legal-tender notes than any other system of paper money with which I am acquainted. Not only were they a legal tender, but they were declared to be redeemable in land; each note bearing a certain daily interest, and entitling the holder to confiscated lots equal in value to the face of the note, just as our early notes entitled the holders to certain United States bonds. At first the new scheme worked well, as such schemes always do. The people were delighted to be freed from the visits of the tax-gatherer. The assignats paid off the public creditors, purchased army supplies, and kept the Government going. They furnished the people with money, the great national want. Very soon, however, the other side of the picture began to be seen. All the necessaries of life gradually rose in price. There was an almost total stoppage of productive industry, everybody trying to make money in any other way than by regular work. The Convention, backed by the mob and by the guillotine, vainly endeavored to fix a maximum of prices. Bakers who refused to sell their loaves at the old prices had their heads cut off and carried through the streets on poles by the mob; but the only result was to make bread still more scarce by frightening the bakers from their work.

So great did the evil become, that in the year 1796, in the very midst of the first Italian campaign, when the twenty years' struggle of France with the other European powers was but just fairly begun, the paper money had to be entirely withdrawn and its place filled by coin. If our theories of the necessity of paper money are correct, this downfall of the circulating medium must have been disastrous in the extreme. But so far was this from being the case, that productive industry rapidly recovered from the depression of the paper money. Men raised grain and made bread in the full confidence that no mob would punish them for their pains by compelling them to part with it for worthless rags. The war was continued nineteen years without any attempt to issue more paper money; and in the only instance since that time in which irredeemable bills have been allowed to circulate in France, their amount was carefully limited so as to be insufficient for the purposes of currency, and thus necessitate the circulation of more or less specie.

LESSON XIII.

THE PUBLIC FAITH.

"MORE greenbacks," "The dollar of our fathers," and "The repeal of the Resumption Act," are, at the present time, three loud cries, which we hear on all sides. What is meant by the second cry, however, is not really the dollar of our fathers, but a certain silver dollar which for forty years has been unknown in commerce. The advocates of this dollar claim that the repeal of the law making it a legal tender in the year 1873 was a great wrong. In making this claim, they tacitly assume that the dollar was in use previous to that time, and that by thus demonetizing it a portion of the money power of the country was withdrawn. In fact, however, for the last two generations the gold dollar has been cheaper than the silver one; so that the latter was not really in use at all. The act complained of was nothing more than the acceptance of a fixed fact, the fact that the silver dollar had gone out of use. Not one word of this cry would ever have been heard had it not been for the recent immense fall in the price of silver. The very fact that the dollar has been unknown in commerce for more than forty years is itself one of the strongest possible reasons against reviving it. Another strong reason is, that to revive it would be simply taking the cast-off money of Germany to use ourselves. But the strongest reason of all is found in the fact that gold is immensely better, and more convenient material for making money in large sums, than silver is. Of course, for all small payments silver has been used, and will continue to be used; but when we come to payments involving thousands of dollars, the silver is entirely too cumbrous to be conveniently handled, and is, besides, less durable than gold. The superiority of gold is so obvious that the only real reason for favoring the silver dollar is, firstly, that it is now the cheapest one; and, secondly, that its introduction would tend to make specie payments more difficult. In the second reason, the whole question which we are considering is involved. We shall therefore not consider it at present. Respecting the first, we shall only say that a cheap dollar merely means a dollar which will not buy you so much food and clothing. When the men who live by wages once fully understand that this is the reason why the silver dollar is recommended to them rather than the gold one, very little further argument will be necessary.

The issue of greenbacks, and cheap money generally, is frequently supported on the ground that we shall thus have an instrument with which to discharge debts, and that the more plentiful this instrument, the more readily will the debts be discharged. Those who think thus seem to think paying a debt is a mere matter of form which a person has to go through, and there is an end to it. If we look at it a little closer, we shall see that the payment of a debt is the fulfilment of a contract in which we are to be guided, not by any mere form, but by the intent and meaning of the contract itself. The fact that one person may have made a bad bargain, and may suffer by having to fulfil it, is no reason whatever for annulling it. Now, to issue more greenbacks and new kinds of dollars, in order to enable debtors more easily to fulfil their promises to pay money to their creditors, would be as complete a fraud as it would to take a lot of cornmeal, pass a law calling it first-class family flour, and pass it off on the consumer in fulfilment of a contract to sell him the latter sort of flour. Every contract to pay money made during the last eight years has been made with the legal understanding that it

might have to be paid in gold or its equivalent.

In 1869, the Congress of the United States passed a solemn act pledging the faith of the Government to provide for the payment of its notes in coin. As many of my readers may not have seen this law, I will here quote the provisions bearing on legal-tender notes from the Revised Statutes of the United States:

"The faith of the United States is solemnly pledged to the payment, in coin or its equivalent, of all the obligations of the United States not bearing interest known as United States notes. * * * The faith of the United States is also solemnly pledged to make provisions at the earliest practicable period for the redemption of the United States notes in coin."—*Revised Statutes of the United States*, p. 735.

In pursuance of this solemn pledge, Congress, in January, 1875, provided for resuming specie payments on January 1st, 1879. I think I have sufficiently shown that the highest interest of the country in all its departments demands this policy.

But, interest aside, the solemn faith of the Government is pledged to it, and the law cannot be repealed without a most gross breach of that faith against which no amount of merely material advantage could be placed. Every man who since that time has incurred a debt, has incurred it knowing that, when it became due, the paper in which he paid it would, by the law of the land, be redeemable in gold coin.

During the interval referred to, the rate of interest has been lower than it ever was before in this country, owing to this very expectation of resumption of specie payments. It is the debtor's own fault if he find that he must now pay more valuable dollars than he expected to. If you are a debtor, you say, perhaps, that you did not expect that specie payments really would be resumed and the gold dollar again come into use. If so, you are simply pitting your own interests against those of society. Your position is very much like that of one of a large number of persons who have given their promissory notes for a much greater amount than value received,

under the impression that there was a fair chance of their never being collected. You and I would both be very sorry for those who had taken so heavy a risk on the assumption that law was not to take its course; but that would not be any reason for refusing payment of their notes.

To prevent a possible misapprehension, it must be remembered that resumption does not mean contraction of the currency, and does not of necessity involve any contraction. All it requires is, that Government shall stand ready to redeem the promise printed on the face of every greenback, if the holder desires it: if he does not desire it, but prefers using the note as money, no law will compel him to exchange it for gold. If the total amount of currency in circulation does not exceed the wants of business, none will be sent in for redemption, and there will be no contraction; but if there is more than is really necessary, then the excess will be gradually sent in. And we must never forget that the more certain redemption is to be the permanent policy of the Government, the less owners of currency will send for redemption. The great facts and principles of sound currency can in great part be condensed into three sentences.

1. The experience of the whole human race in all ages shows that exchangeable value can reside only in things which men desire to possess, and that, among the various articles of desire, gold and silver are those best adapted to answer for use as money—the former for large payments, the latter for small ones.

2. Under no circumstances should any paper tokens be allowed to circulate as money except those with which the holder can obtain their face value in gold and silver whenever he wishes it.

3. So long as the payment of all paper money in gold at the pleasure of the holder is well secured, there is no necessity of placing a fixed limit upon its volume.

LESSON XIV.

THE CAUSE AND THE REMEDY.

The Cause.

THAT the present state of the labor of the country exhibits some distressing features, no one denies. No one will refuse his assent to any measure which will really and permanently relieve it without bringing on greater evils in the future. If we can form some idea of the causes of the present state of things, we shall be better able to judge of the remedy.

No doubt, one of the principal causes is to be found in those inevitable fluctuations of business and of industry which have always been the common experience of civilized men. At one time business is brisk; every one is employed; wages are high; and men generally are happy. In the course of a few years an era of depression sets in; capital ceases to make any profit; wages are lowered, and laborers find themselves suffering for want of the necessaries of life. These fluctuations, I say, are simply inevitable, and there is no remedy against them except to patiently fight them through, in the full consciousness that as times have improved after every such depression heretofore, they will improve in the future.

But in our own case the depression is no doubt aggravated by two other causes: the first of these is, we fought a great war very largely on borrowed money, and for more than ten years we have been largely living and developing our resources by borrowing. It is estimated that a large proportion of the public debt of the country is now held in Europe. Every bond that we have sent to Europe has been sent in payment for some service or commodity received from there for us to add to our resources. In other words, we have practically been running in debt to Europe, and living beyond our income for a period of some fifteen years. Now, this practice of living beyond one's income is something which must inevitably come to a stop, whether practised by a nation or by an individual; and it is something the stoppage of which is always accompanied by distress.

The second cause to which I allude is our irredeemable paper currency. The history of paper money in this and other countries, when issued in quantities greater than could be redeemed, exhibits some common features. The first effect always is to introduce an era of seeming prosperity. Notwithstanding that it has hardly ever been issued except in times which would otherwise be considered as times of great national distress, such as an exhausting war, it has always produced an amount of extravagant expenditure which would otherwise be impossible. The blood seems to course through the veins of the body politic at a rate never before known. It was so in our colonial times; it was so in the French Revolution; it was so during our Revolutionary War, and, to a certain extent, during and following our Civil War, although its stimulating effect was then less felt, because the issues were not made with the extravagance which generally characterizes this policy. Still, there was some such effect, as was seen in the almost entire absence of depression during the period immediately following the war. The depression we might have experienced was greatly diminished by the constant export of our Government bonds to Europe in payment for goods. But the depression must come, sooner or later. The nation which indulges in paper money acts exactly on the principle of the man who indulges in drink. First, we have stimulation; then, depression, which the victim thinks he can overcome only by more drink.

Again, the policy of specie resumption and the gradual appreciation of the currency seemingly increase the difficulty, just as total abstinence on the part of the man who has been long indulging in drink gives great temporary distress. It is, no doubt, in the combination of all these causes that we are to look for the source of the depression of business at the present time.

The Remedy.

When the caravan is passing over the Desert of Sahara, it is not uncommon for its thirsty souls to be deceived by the mirage. At a few miles' distance they see what seems to be a lake of clear water; and, leaving their road to go and quench their thirst, they are led on and on, only to find themselves the victims of the bitterest delusion. The remedy for the present difficulties now most strongly urged upon us is of this character. It is to depreciate the currency, and give up all that we have gained in the direction of specie payments during the past ten years, by issuing a larger supply of greenbacks. Undoubtedly, such a policy would for the moment please a large body of the more thoughtless class, who would again find themselves receiving two or three, or perhaps ten, dollars a day for their work. Their joy would be very much like that of the men who had just left their caravan to go in search of the mirage, and who think they see the water they are to drink only a few hundred yards away. The result would be that the laborer would soon find that his two or three or ten dollars would buy him no more food and clothing than would fifty cents, for which he had before refused to work; and he would be then just as badly off as if his wages had in the beginning been reduced to fifty cents a day. And then, as an end must come at last, the end of it all would be a depression much greater than that which we now suffer, and the consciousness of a dishonored national faith in the bargain, besides a blow to our public credit and our national prosperity, from which it would take a whole generation to recover. The true course is directly the opposite. The surest and quickest road to general prosperity is to be found in immediate resumption. The difficulties of the present crisis are greatly aggravated by the uncertainty which hangs over the future. Nobody is yet quite certain that we are really coming to specie payments, and everybody is more or less fearful, or some, perhaps we might say, are more or less hopeful, that before 1879 unlimited greenbacks will be the order of the day. So long as this uncertainty exists, it is absolutely impossible for the business of the country to go into operation on a really healthy and settled basis. But when it is once undoubtedly established that the only legal dollar is the honest gold dollar, the dollar made of the only material which the experience of all countries, through thousands of years, has shown to be always effective, then every one will know exactly on what basis he is to go. The laborer will then be satisfied with wages which, compared with those of the last ten years, may be low, because he will know that, when paid in honest gold, they will buy him more of the necessaries of life. But the millennium will not be inaugurated. Progress is necessarily slow and gradual; and no arrangement which can possibly be made will secure to people in general better food and clothing, or houses, than those which on the average they have enjoyed during the past twenty years.

Meanwhile, privations must be patiently borne, and the difficulties which beset us must be gradually worked away. The more ready the laboring classes are to accept the inevitable low wages of the present time, and to work for whatever their employers are able to pay them, the more quickly will better times come. The inauguration of strikes at the present time is like bleeding a man who is just beginning to recuperate from the prostrating effects of sickness.

Let us now bring together the reasons why the policy of inflating the currency in any way should be condemned, and why the policy of resumption should be carried out.

1. All experience shows that gold and silver form the only stable basis for any system of currency. Gold always has been, now is, and for generations to come will continue to be, the standard of value for the whole world, no matter how many paper dollars we may issue.

2. Repeated laws of Congress have pledged the national faith to all creditors that its legal-tender notes should be paid in coin; and the repeal of those laws would be an act of the grossest national dishonor, having no other result than the legalized robbery of one class of the community for the benefit of another class.

3. The only way to permanently relieve ourselves from our present financial difficulties is to take such measures that every laborer in the land shall receive his wages, be they low or high, in honest gold and silver, or in notes convertible into gold.

4. By continued resumption, we shall be saved from having again to suffer the evils of a depreciated currency; whereas, to now take a backward step would be to plunge into them again, and to go once more through all the difficulties we are now encountering.

LESSON XV.

SOME GENERAL THOUGHTS.

This question of regulating the currency is no easy one, to be settled by an off-hand opinion even of wise men, much less of men entirely ignorant of the history and laws of the subject. It perplexes the best intellects of the world, and will probably continue to do so for a long time to come.

It is so intricate that only a mathematical head can unravel it—the same kind of a head which can solve a tough problem in algebra, or settle the accounts of the Tweed Ring, and tell just how much money each man owes. Neither fine writing nor oratory will afford the slightest help, any more than it will help a man to understand a steam-engine.

The advocates of redeemable money have no millennium to offer. They know that the sentence, "In the sweat of thy face shalt thou eat bread," cannot be commuted by any human contrivance; that there is no real value which can be commanded by any other agency than labor of the hand or head. They perfectly know the difficulties which beset any system of redemption of paper in coin, and are as keenly alive to them, and as anxious to remedy them, as the strongest paper-money advocates can be. But they know also that to undertake to avoid these difficulties by doing away with redemption in gold is as foolish as if the passengers in a ship, finding that she was tossed by the storm, frightfully beaten by the waves, and in danger of destruction, should scuttle her and take to swimming, for fear of suffering shipwreck. I think most readers must have a faint suspicion that the wisest of the human race are opposed to irredeemable paper. If you were to take a vote of the political economists, the close students, the bankers, the professors, and the historians on the subject—in fine, of all those men who, either by their knowledge or their powers of investigation, are best fitted to understand the subject, the vote for irredeemable currency would be astonishingly small. If the reader distrusts his own judgment, this fact is worth thinking of.

We can hardly conceive a scene of more dramatic interest than that of the people of our country preparing to decide whether they will taste the tempting cup which the advocates of inflation are holding to their lips, and accept the honeyed words in which they are told that it contains the magic elixir of life, which will put money into every poor man's pocket. A hundred generations of the human race have held their breath as they have heard or read the song of the sirens addressed to Ulysses, which would have allured him to destruction if he had not filled the ears of his crew with wax:

"Oh stay, O pride of Greece, Ulysses, stay;
Oh cease thy course, and listen to our lay.
Blest is the man ordained our voice to hear;
The song instructs the soul and charms the ear.
Approach! thy soul shall into raptures rise;
Approach! and learn new wisdom from the wise.
We know whate'er the kings of mighty name
Achieved at Ilion in the field of fame,
Whate'er beneath the sun's bright journey lies.
Oh stay, and learn new wisdom from the wise!"

The drunkard, holding the intoxicating cup to the lips of the innocent boy, and saying, "Just swallow this, my boy, and your thirst will be quenched—you will feel new life in your veins, new strength in your limbs, and a happiness in your spirits of which you never dreamed," affords the moralist a scene on which he has dwelt ever since the days of Solomon. The present crisis in our national history is similar to that in the life of Ulysses when the song of the sirens charmed his soul, or in the life of the boy when he has to decide whether he will taste the cup. The promises are as fair as those of the sirens, the words as tempting as those of the drunkard; the result, a disaster to our national prosperity from which it would take long, long years to recover.

THE END.

Macaulay's Life and Letters.

The Life and Letters of Lord Macaulay. By his Nephew, G. OTTO TREVELYAN, M.P. With Portrait. 2 vols., 8vo, Cloth, uncut edges and gilt tops, $5 00; Sheep, $6 00; Half Calf, $9 50. Popular Edition, 1 vol., 12mo, Cloth, $1 75.

The biography is in every respect worthy of the subject. Mr. Trevelyan has executed his task with most praiseworthy modesty and good taste, and with great literary skill. * * * Macaulay's Life forms a most interesting book, living as he did in the thick of the literary and political activity of his time. It affords us many fresh pictures of incidents in which he played a part, and amusing and instructive anecdotes of the celebrities with whom he came in contact, and, above all, it throws a great deal of unexpected light on his own personal character. * * * Nothing could surpass the charm of those portions of the biography in which Mr. Trevelyan pictures Macaulay at home, from the time when, already a man in learning, he romanced with his playmates on Clapham Common, to the time when, still a boy in animal spirits, he wrote to his sisters, from the smoking-room of the House of Commons, exuberantly lively and brilliant descriptions of the great Reform debates, or spent evenings with them in Great Ormond Street, punning, reciting, and capping verses, in the intervals between his astonishing the House with displays of oratory which excelled every thing heard "since Plunket;" or, later still, when, in the intervals of composing his history, he took his nephews and nieces with him on holiday tours, and kept them in fits of laughter with puns, rhymes, and tales, from one end of a railway journey to the other.—*Examiner*, London.

Published by HARPER & BROTHERS, New York.

☞ HARPER & BROTHERS *will send the above work by mail, postage prepaid, to any part of the United States or Canada, on receipt of the price.*

www.ingramcontent.com/pod-product-compliance
Lightning Source LLC
LaVergne TN
LVHW021420110826
845150LV00007B/2006

* 9 7 8 1 4 2 5 5 0 8 6 7 8 *